EXPLORE SPRING!

25 Great Ways to Learn About Spring

nomad press

green press
INITIATIVE

Nomad Press is committed to preserving ancient forests
and natural resources. We elected to print *Explore Spring*
on 50% post consumer recycled paper, processed chlorine
free. As a result, for this printing, we have saved:

12 Trees (40' tall and 6-8" diameter)
4,921 Gallons of Wastewater
1,979 Kilowatt Hours of Electricity
542 Pounds of Solid Waste
1,066 Pounds of Greenhouse Gases

Nomad Press made this paper choice because our printer,
Thomson-Shore, Inc., is a member of Green Press Initiative, a nonprofit program dedicated to supporting authors,
publishers, and suppliers in their efforts to reduce their use
of fiber obtained from endangered forests.

For more information, visit www.greenpressinitiative.org

Many thanks to Patricia Murray for her insightful comments and advice.

Contents

Other titles in Explore Your World! series

Let's Investigate Spring!

ook outside, it's spring! Birds are building nests. Flowers are blooming. Trees have new, green leaves. And everywhere, animals have new babies to raise.

Spring is a time of new life. It is a time when the world outside wakes up from winter. The days get longer and warmer. But why do we have spring, and why does it happen at the same time every year?

This book is going to take a careful look at spring—the season between winter and summer. As you read this book you'll see that spring is a time when the outdoor environment changes almost every day.

You'll get to do lots of experiments and projects to see those changes up close. You'll find out some interesting stuff. And you'll learn a lot of silly jokes and amazing facts, too. So get ready to step out of your snow boots and into your mud boots and learn about the season of spring!

Be a Scientist!

Most of the projects and activities in this book will have you ask questions and then try to come up with the answers: that's what scientists call the **scientific process**. It's the way scientists learn and study the world around them. What's really interesting about the scientific process is that you can't just ask a question, answer it, and then be done. You have to prove every answer you give so other people can get the same answer using the same method you did.

Here's how the scientific process works:

1 You ask a question or have an idea about something, called a **hypothesis**.

 **2** Then you come up with ways, or **experiments** to answer the question or prove your idea.

 **3** You do the experiment to see if you can prove your idea.

 **4** You change your idea based on the result of your experiment.

Scientists of all Kinds

A **scientist** is a person who studies nature or the universe, or a part of nature or the universe. A scientist can study something as large as the sun, or as small as atoms. One thing you might notice is that many branches of science end in "ology," like zoology, or biology. Ology means "the study of." It comes from an ancient language called Greek. Many of the names for different types of scientists also come from Greek. For example, if you are a scientist who studies animals, you study zoology. If you study snakes, you are interested in herpetology. Herpeton is a Greek word, which means "to creep." That's a pretty good name for studying snakes, right? Can you think of some other scientific names that end in "ology?"

WOW! For about 500 years now, the season after winter has been called "spring" because plants seem to spring from the earth. Many, many years ago, people used to call the season after winter "lenten." Lenten used to describe how the days were getting longer, or lengthening. Lengthen, Lenten—get it?

What else do scientists do?

collect

Scientists **collect:** they gather things to observe them.

observe

Scientists **observe:** they look at things carefully and notice what changes and what stays the same.

sort

Scientists **sort:** they organize the things they gather into different groups.

Words 2 Know

spring: the season in between winter and summer, from about March 21 to June 21 in the Northern Hemisphere and from about September 22 to December 21 in the Southern Hemisphere.

scientific process: the way scientists ask questions and do experiments to try to prove their ideas.

hypothesis: an unproven idea that tries to explain certain facts or observations.

experiment: testing an idea.

scientist: someone who studies science and knows a lot about it.

Make a Science Journal

One thing you'll do to find the answers to your questions is look at things very carefully to see how they are changing. Then you'll write down the changes you notice. Many scientists use a science journal to keep track of what they see. You can do this, too. Any notebook will work for a science journal, even just a few sheets of paper to write down what you see and do. You don't need anything fancy. But if you

continued on next page >>

Supplies

10 pieces of 8½-by-14-inch white paper

large brown grocery bag

ruler

scissors

2 pieces of cardboard like a cracker box or cereal box

glue stick, paste, or white glue

2 pieces colored paper like old wrapping paper, cut to 6 by 8 inches

markers, colored pencils, stickers

hole punch

3 brads or 3 rubber bands

would like to make a special science journal, here's a fun way using an old paper bag, some cardboard, and wrapping paper. When you're done your journal will look like it is covered in tree bark! Since you need to use scissors and a hole punch for this activity, make sure you have a grownup around to help.

1 Fold the pieces of white paper in half. Now you will have paper that is 8½ by 7 inches.

2 Cut the brown paper bag into two 8½-by-10-inch pieces. Crumple, crush, and roll the paper bag sheets so they soften up. As you roll and crumple the paper, the fibers will get as soft as cloth material. Be gentler with the paper as it becomes softer. Spread the pieces out flat.

3 Cut the pieces of cardboard into 7-by-9-inch rectangles. Put glue on one side of each of the cardboard pieces. It doesn't matter which side because you will cover it up.

4 With the gluey side down, center each carboard piece on one of the pieces of brown paper. Push down on the cardboard to make sure it sticks tight to the brown paper.

5 Make a diagonal cut from each brown paper corner to each cardboard corner. Snip off a bit of the brown paper corner. This will make it easy to fold the extra brown paper over the cardboard. Put glue on the extra brown paper surrounding the cardboard and fold it over onto the cardboard on all four sides.

6 Put glue on one side of the colored paper, on the back side if there is a difference. With the gluey side down, center the colored paper over the cardboard. This will cover up the rest of the cardboard and make a nice inside lining to your cover. Your cover is ready to decorate with markers, colored pencils, or stickers.

7 Use the hole punch to punch three holes about one inch from the fold on the white paper. These will be your journal pages. Make sure the holes are in about the same place on all 10 sheets of paper. It doesn't have to be exact. The holes go on the left of your journal.

8 Put the folded white paper inside the front and back covers of your journal. Mark on the inside of the covers where the holes in the paper are.

9 Punch matching holes in the cover so when you put the paper inside the covers you can see straight through all of them.

10 If you are using brads to complete your journal, you can fit them in each hole and fasten them onto the back cover. If you are using rubber bands, put one end of the rubber band through each hole and pull it through the other end of the rubber band. That will hold it tight. You can also use yarn, string, or even a cut-up shoelace!

The Sun Makes the Seasons!

Chapter 1

How can you tell that spring has come to where you live? Well, the weather turns warmer. If you live where it snows, the snow melts and the grass begins to grow.

But sometimes weather plays tricks on us. For example, in the late winter it might be as warm as a spring day for a whole week. Sometimes winter weather comes back just when you thought winter was over. If we can't always rely on the weather to tell us spring has arrived, what can we rely on? The length of the day. As winter turns to spring, the day gets longer. In fact, spring is when we have the longest days of the whole year.

WOW! The weather at the equator, the imaginary line that runs right around the middle of the earth, doesn't change very much all year round. That's because the equater gets the same amount of sun all the time.

The earth has an imaginary line around it called the **equator** that divides the earth into two parts: the **Northern Hemisphere** and the **Southern Hemisphere**. Two times a year the equator is lined up directly with the sun. This happens on the first day of spring and on the first day of fall. On these days, usually March 20 or 21 and September 22 or 23, every point on the earth has 12 hours of sunlight and 12 hours of darkness. This is called the **equinox**.

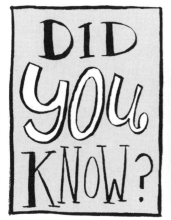

To you and me the earth seems pretty big.

But compared to the sun the earth is small.

Hi there big fella!

↑ Earth   ↑ Sun

In fact the sun is so big ONE MILLION earths could fit inside it.

sun

room for 1,000,000 earths

Amazing sun facts

1 The sun's outer surface is 10,000 degrees Fahrenheit.

2 The earth is 93 million miles away from the sun.

3 The heat from the sun takes 8½ minutes to reach earth.

4 If you drove in a car at 65 miles an hour and never took a break, it would take 163 years to travel to the sun.

5 If you hopped in a jet that traveled 500 miles an hour it would still take 21 years to reach the sun!

THE BIG IDEA: Why the Earth Has Seasons

You may live in a place where it is warm all year round. Or you may live in a place where it is cold in the winter, hot in the summer, and warm in the spring and fall. No matter where you live, your place on planet earth experiences four seasons. The four seasons are spring, summer, winter, and fall, and the reason we earthlings have seasons has to do with the way the earth moves around the sun.

winter — shorter days

spring — longer days

The earth travels slowly around the sun all the time. The sun is so big that it takes about 365 days for the earth to complete one full circle around the sun. We call that amount of time a year. While the earth moves around the sun, it spins like a top that is tilted to one side. Only part of the earth can be tilted toward the sun at once. Whichever part of the earth is tilted toward the sun is having summer. It is getting more direct sunlight than the part of the earth tilted away from the sun. And guess what? The part tilted away is having winter! In between summer and winter, when the part of the earth tilted away from the sun moves to being tilted toward the sun, you get spring.

When it is summer in the Northern Hemisphere the North Pole is the closest point on earth to the sun but it is still cold. That is true for the South Pole when it is summer in the Southern Hemisphere, too. What does this prove? That the distance from the earth to the sun isn't what determines how warm it gets. Warmth is caused by the angle and amount of sunlight.

Even though the North and South Poles get 24 hours of sunlight in their summer, they remain cold because the sunlight is not very direct. Also for half the year the poles get little or no sunlight. It gets so cold at the poles during this time that it never warms up, even in summer. And what about the weather near the equator? It doesn't change very much all year round. That's because it gets the same amount of direct sunlight all the time.

Words 2 Know

equator: the imaginary line running around the middle of the earth that divides it in two halves.

Northern Hemisphere: the half of the earth to the north of the equator.

Southern Hemisphere: the half of the earth to the south of the equator.

equinox: two times a year when everywhere has exactly 12 hours of daylight and 12 hours of darkness.

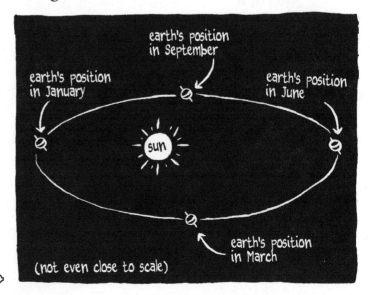

earth's position in September

earth's position in January

earth's position in June

sun

earth's position in March

(not even close to scale)

Shedding Some Light on the Seasons

This activity will show why summer days are warmer than winter days, all because of the tilt of the earth as it moves around the sun.

1 Turn on the flashlight in a dark room. Hold it so the beam is shining straight down onto the flat surface. You should be able to see a bright circle of light. This is what the sunlight is like in the summer, strong and direct.

2 Now turn the flashlight so the beam of light is at an angle. Can you see how much more area the light has to cover when it is tilted? Can you see that it's not as bright? That's the same thing that happens to the sun in winter. The light is not as direct. It has to travel over a much wider area and becomes weaker.

Supplies

dark room
flat surface
flashlight

The Sun Makes the Seasons!

Is it spring everywhere?

The seasons are caused by the earth's path around the sun. Every place on earth has seasons. But on different parts of the planet, the seasons are a bit different. If you live near the equator, called the tropics, you probably won't notice a big change in the temperature during a year. That makes sense, because the equator is the part of the earth that gets about the same amount of sunlight no matter what time of year it is. This means that the temperatures stay pretty much the same all year.

So what kinds of seasons do the tropics have? Rainy seasons and dry seasons. Just as people who live in the northern part of the world can plan on warmer air and green buds in the months between April and June, people in the tropics north of the equator can plan on those months being rainy. The rainy season in the northern tropics usually lasts from around April or May to September or October. The dry season lasts from October to March or April. If you want to spend spring in the tropics, don't forget your umbrella! It is the other way around in the tropics south of the equator.

At the top and bottom of the earth are the North and South Poles. In the summer, it never gets dark at the pole tilted toward the sun. And in the winter, it never gets light at the pole tilted away from the sun. Would you like to live where it never gets dark for weeks at a time?

Making Some

How does the tilt of the earth and the way it spins like a top while it circles the sun affect how much sunlight different parts get? It's much easier to understand when you see it in action!

1 Draw a line around the middle of your orange. That line will be the equator.

2 Put one thumbtack or sticker on the top of the orange and one thumbtack or sticker on the bottom. These will help you remember the Northern (top) and Southern (bottom) Hemispheres.

3 Hold your orange so your equator is parallel to the floor. Now push one toothpick into the top and another toothpick into the bottom of your orange. These are your North and South Poles. Push the toothpicks far enough into the orange so that you can hold the toothpicks and spin the orange around. One time around is a day.

Sense of the Spin

4 Put the large bowl upside down on a small table for your sun. The sun is much, much bigger compared to the earth than this, of course. Mark a starting point on the bowl.

5 Hold the orange by the toothpicks. Tilt the orange so the bottom toothpick, your South Pole, is slightly tilted toward the bowl, your sun. Slowly move the orange around the bowl. At the same time, spin the orange around itself while keeping it tilted.

As you first spin the orange around itself and also circle the bowl, you'll see that the bottom half of the orange (the Southern Hemisphere) faces the sun more directly. But what happens when you get about halfway around the bowl? The upper part of the orange, the Northern Hemisphere, faces the sun more directly. That's just what happens to the earth as it moves around the sun. Part of the year the Northern Hemisphere faces the sun more directly and has summer, and part of the year the Southern Hemisphere faces the sun more directly. In between, neither hemisphere faces the sun more directly and they have spring or fall.

Supplies

an orange
black marker
2 thumbtacks or stickers of different colors
2 toothpicks
a large bowl

Green, Green, Green!

Chapter 2

No matter where you live, spring is the season of the year when plants grow the most every day. Have you ever noticed how green it gets in the spring? Green is all around you. Why?

In the spring, more of the sun's energy reaches the earth. The sunlight is getting more and more direct. More sunlight means warmer soil. As the soil warms up, water frozen in the soil melts. More sunlight also means warmer oceans, which 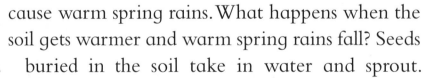 cause warm spring rains. What happens when the soil gets warmer and warm spring rains fall? Seeds buried in the soil take in water and sprout.

Soil is made of rocks, leaves, bugs, and other living stuff...

Over time rocks break down...

crack

into smaller and smaller pieces.

The very small pieces of rock mix with living and dead material that has fallen to the ground, and combines to make **SOIL.**

SOIL

These sprouts turn into green plants with leaves that reach for the sun and roots that spread down through the soil.

Soil: It's Not Just a Bunch of Dirt

Soil is the top layer of the earth's surface. Soil is made of lots of different things. Look at it closely. Soil has rocks, clay, sand, leaves, worms, and bugs in it. The soil in your yard can be different from the soil in your best friend's yard. And it changes all the time. Over very long periods of time, rocks break down into teeny, tiny pieces. They mix with living and dead material that falls to the ground every year, like leaves, bits of wood, and grass, even dead animals and insects.

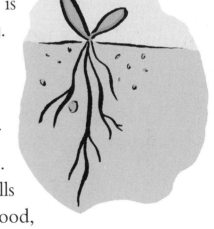

WOW! Different parts of the earth have different kinds of soil. It depends on what plants grow there, what kinds of rocks that part of the earth has, and the climate.

17

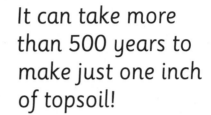

WOW! It can take more than 500 years to make just one inch of topsoil!

Bacteria and fungus are also in the soil, so small you can't see them. Along with worms and ants, these tiny things help break down leaves and grass and other dead things into smaller pieces that mix together and add to the soil.

Soil is porous. That means there are lots of itty bitty spaces in between the pieces of rocks, leaves, bugs, and other stuff. Those spaces are important for plants because that is where water and air collect in the soil. Plants need both water and air in the soil to grow well. A lot of sand in soil makes it really porous. That can make the soil dry out very quickly, so plants dry out, too.

Arctic Plants Grow Sideways!

Only the top few inches of soil thaws in the Arctic during the spring. Plant roots in the Arctic have to grow sideways, instead of growing down, since so much of the soil is permanently frozen. This permanently frozen soil is called permafrost. That's one reason that the trees in the Arctic are so short. The tallest trees are only about 6 feet tall because shallow roots can't support very tall trees.

The Great Spring Soil Warm Up

How does the soil warm up in the spring? See for yourself.

1 Find a spot of bare soil on the sunniest side of your school or house. This will probably be on the south side. This spot should get a lot of spring sunshine.

2 Find another spot of bare soil under a tree or in an area that doesn't get much sun, maybe on the north side.

3 Check the soil temperature at both locations the same time once a week starting in March or April and ending in June.

4 Make a chart for your data in your science journal and compare the temperature of the soil in both spots.

Supplies

2 soil thermometers
(from any garden center)

your science journal

Things to notice

❀ Did the soil heat up slowly or quickly over time?

❀ Did the soil in one area warm up faster than the other?

❀ What did you notice about the surface of the soil at the different temperatures?

❀ Did the surface of the soil in one spot change faster or more than the other?

Sunflowers Really Like the Sun

Sunflowers are tall plants with very large brown and yellow blossoms. You might think they are called sunflowers because their blooms look a bit like a sun. But the real reason sunflowers got their name is that those big blooms actually follow the sun across its path during the day. On a sunny day watch a sunflower in the morning and notice the direction its blossom faces. Look at the sunflower a few hours later and write down where the flower is pointing. Then look at the sunflower a few hours after that and write down where the flower faces now. You should be able to catch the sunflower in action!

Words 2 Know

germination: when a seed opens and starts to grow toward light.

chlorophyll: the chemical inside plant leaves that helps them make food.

photosynthesis: the way a plant makes its own food.

capillary action: the way plants pull water up from the soil into their leaves.

A lot of clay in soil makes it less porous. That can make the soil very heavy so plant roots have a hard time pushing through. Clay soil also makes it hard for water to drain through it easily. The best soil for plants is not too dry or and not too wet. That's the kind plants like best!

In the winter, the water in the soil freezes. In the spring, this water thaws. What is really interesting is that not all the water in soil freezes and unfreezes at exactly the same time. This is because soil in different places is made of different material and receives different amounts

of sunlight. Why is the freezing and unfreezing of soil so important? Because as the ice in soil melts it waters the seeds buried in it, and the soil gets soft enough for the roots to grow and spread.

Plants Sprout In the Spring

Every plant seed has the beginnings of a plant curled up inside of it. Food for the plant is also stored inside the seed. The seed is covered by a seed coat that keeps the plant inside warm and protected until the conditions are right for it to grow. In the spring, the soil is warmed by the sun, and the water that was frozen in the soil melts. The warm, wet soil makes the seed coat swell until it bursts open under ground. This is called **germination**.

21

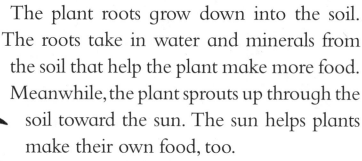

The plant roots grow down into the soil. The roots take in water and minerals from the soil that help the plant make more food. Meanwhile, the plant sprouts up through the soil toward the sun. The sun helps plants make their own food, too.

What happens once plants have broken through the surface of the soil? They sprout leaves. Plants take in the sun through their leaves and begin to make their own food. A chemical inside of plants, called **chlorophyll**, traps the sun's energy and makes plants green. Through a process called **photosynthesis**, plants turn this energy into food.

Summer Slumber

Why does everything grow so much in spring, but not as much during the summer? Because all through spring the days are getting longer. Longer days mean more sunlight and more photosynthesis. The longest day of the year for the Northern Hemisphere is June 21. This is the first day of summer. But guess what? Even though it continues to get hotter in summer, each day gets shorter than the one before it. Shorter days mean less sun and less photosynthesis. Less photosynthesis means less growth for plants.

The more sun a plant gets, the more food it makes for itself and the bigger it grows. That's why plants go so crazy in the spring when there is more sunlight for longer periods of time. Can you imagine how big you'd grow every spring if you were made of chlorophyll? Yikes!

Seeds on Fire

Most seeds sprout when the soil is damp and warm, but some seeds can only sprout in the heat of a forest fire! In the western United States, plants called chaparral only sprout after they have been exposed to the high temperatures and the smoke of a forest fire. Some seeds of the chaparral will stay in the soil for years, waiting for a fire to come and help them sprout.

WOW! The biggest flower in the world grows on the island of Sumatra. It can be 4 feet across, 10 feet tall, and weigh 25 pounds. It also smells like rotting fish. Yuck!

The Great Sprout Race

How do plants grow in spring? The best way to learn is to sprout some plants for yourself.

1 Roll up the 2 pieces of black construction paper and slide one into each jar or cup so it presses against the sides.

2 Add just enough water to cover the bottom. The water should be about a half-inch deep. The paper will slowly absorb the water, giving the seed enough moisture to germinate without drowning it.

3 Put a seed or two in between the jar and the paper in each jar. Place one jar in a warm, sunny place, and the other in a place that is cooler and darker.

4 Keep track of when each seed sprouts. Measure how much each sprout grows every day. Record your data in your science journal.

Just for laughs

Q: Why did the leaf go to the doctor?

A: It was feeling green!

Supplies

2 pieces of black construction paper

water

2 clear plastic cups or glass jars

a few seeds like peas, pumpkin, or beans

your science journal

Things to notice

✿ Did the seeds change shape?

✿ Which seed sprouted first, and why?

✿ Did the seeds grow at the same rate after they sprouted? Why or why not?

✿ Does one seed have longer roots than the other?

✿ What else did you notice about this experiment?

These Seeds are All Wet!

Can some plants grow without soil? Yes, they get their nutrients from water instead. Even some plants that require soil in nature can be grown in water by farmers. This is called hydroponics. Hydroponics only works when farmers add nutrients and protein to the water. This experiment is very similar to the last one, but it will show you the difference between growing plants with and without soil.

1 Roll up the pieces of black construction paper and slide the paper into each jar or cup so it presses against the sides.

2 Add just enough water to cover the bottom of each jar. The water should be about a half-inch deep. The paper will slowly absorb the water, and give the seed enough moisture to germinate without drowning it.

3 Put seeds between the side of the jar and the paper. Put the jars on a sunny windowsill.

4 Check both jars each day. When the seeds have begun to sprout, take one cup and fill it with soil. Keep the soil moist. Add water to the other jar, enough so that the roots are touching the water. Maintain this water level each day. Check both jars after a few days.

Things to notice

✿ How does the seedling in the soil look different from the seedling in the water?

✿ Is the seedling in one container a different size than the seedling in the other?

✿ What are your ideas about soil and plants? Record your notes in your science journal.

Supplies

2 pieces of black construction paper

2 clear plastic cups or glass jars

water

a few seeds like peas, pumpkin, or bean seeds

1 cup of potting soil

your science journal

Some plants, such as the Venus Flytrap, actually eat insects!

They do this because they can't get enough minerals from the soil to make their own food.

mineral rich bugs

poor soil

Plants Drink Water

Did you know that plants drink water from the soil? They don't drink the same way you do. Plant roots carry water from the soil up to their leaves kind of like the way pipes in your house bring water to your faucets. But how does the water get pulled from the soil up to the leaves? First of all, water likes to attach itself to other surfaces, like plant roots. Water droplets also like to attach to other water droplets (water likes hanging out with water!). After enough water gathers together in the plant's roots it needs somewhere else to go, so it climbs up through the roots to the leaves. This process is happening all the time in a plant, and it is called **capillary action**.

Carnation Creation

Here is a really fun way to watch capillary action in action.

1 Snip the bottom inch off of each carnation.
Fill three glasses with water.

2 Put 10 to 20 drops of food coloring in each glass. One glass gets green, one glass gets blue, and one glass gets red.

3 Put a carnation in each glass. Let them sit overnight. Record your observations in your science journal.

Supplies

3 white carnations

scissors

3 glasses

water

green, blue, and red food coloring

your science journal

Things to notice

✿ Before you started, what did you think was going to happen to the food coloring? Write your hypothesis in your science journal.

✿ What happened to the white carnations?

✿ Did they change color? If so, why do you think that is the case?

✿ Did one color work better than another?

The Celery Race

Another fun way to watch capillary action is to have a celery stalk race. Have a grownup help with the vegetable peeler.

1 Put four celery stalks side by side on a cutting board. The place on each stalk where the leaves start should match up.

2 Cut the stalks of celery 4 inches below where the stalks and leaves meet. The celery stalks should all be the same length now.

3 Fill the cups with water. Add 10 to 20 drops of food coloring into each cup. Put one celery stalk in each cup with the leaves up.

4 Line up four paper towels. Label the first "2 hours," the next one "4 hours," the third one "6 hours," and the last one "8 hours." Every 2 hours from the time you put the celery into the cups, remove one stalk and put it onto the correct towel.

5 Each time you take a celery stalk out of the water, use the vegetable peeler to take off the outer layer of celery so you can see how far up the stalk the color traveled.

6 When all the celery stalks are out of the water, measure how high up each stalk the color traveled.

Supplies

4 fresh celery stalks with leaves, all about the same size

ruler

knife

4 cups, paper or plastic

water

red or blue food coloring

4 paper towels

vegetable peeler

your science journal

Things to notice

❀ How long did it take for the first celery stalk to change?

❀ Which celery stalk had the most color in it?

❀ What else did you notice?

28

Leave the Leaves

Leaves not only help a plant make its own food. Leaves also help plants collect moisture from the soil. Why? Because more leaves mean more space in a plant for water to go. More space for water to go means more will be collected. In this experiment you'll see if a plant with leaves can move water from the soil better than a plant without leaves.

1 Place the four celery stalks side by side on a cutting board. The place on the stalks where the leaves start should line up.

2 Cut the stalks of celery 4 inches below where the stalks and leaves meet. The celery stalks should all be the same length.

3 Take two of the celery stalks and cut off all of their leaves. All that is left is a bare stalk. Now you'll have two stalks with leaves and two without leaves.

4 Fill the cups with water and add 10 to 20 drops of food coloring into each cup.

5 Put one celery stalk in each cup. Let the celery sit in the colored water for 2 hours, then take the stalks out.

6 Use the vegetable peeler to take off the outer layer of celery so you can see how far the color has traveled.

Things to notice

✿ Which celery stalks collected the most color?

✿ Which collected color the fastest?

✿ Did leaves make it easier or harder for the celery to move water?

✿ What else did you notice about this experiment?

Supplies

4 fresh celery stalks with leaves, the same size

ruler

knife

4 cups

water

red or blue food coloring

vegetable peeler

your science journal

29

Trees & Leaves

Small plants aren't the only green things you'll see outside in the spring. Look up— the trees have new buds and leaves on them, too! Trees can be divided into two groups.

Conifers are trees with cones. Their leaves look like needles. Most conifers are called **evergreen** since they don't lose all of

DID YOU KNOW?

Most woodland wildflowers are the first plants to bloom in the spring.

Since they grow under the trees...

They need to reach the sun before the trees grow leaves that block out the sunlight to the ground.

their leaves or needles each year. Pine trees, firs, cedars, and spruces are conifers. Some conifers aren't evergreens, though. That's because there are some conifers that lose their leaves each year. Larches and bald cypresses have cones and needle-like leaves, but every fall they lose their needles.

Broadleaf trees lose their leaves in the fall. They are often called **deciduous** trees. Broadleaf trees might bear flowers, fruits, or nuts. Oaks, maples, fruit trees, birch, and beech trees are just a few broadleaf trees. Some broadleaf trees that live in warm climates, like magnolias, don't lose all of their leaves at once. They look evergreen, but since they lose their leaves, they aren't.

Words 2 Know

conifer trees: trees that have cones and leaves like needles—most conifers are also evergreen trees.

evergreen trees: trees that don't lose their leaves in the fall and stay green all year round.

deciduous or broadleaf trees: trees that lose their leaves in the fall and grow new ones in the spring.

dormant: when plants are dormant they stop growing for a period of time.

species: an animal or plant family.

31

Broadleaf or Conifer?

In this activity you will investigate what kind of trees are in your yard or in a nearby park.

1 Make a checklist in your science journal that lists what makes a tree a conifer, and what makes a tree a broadleaf.

Conifer:
needle-like or scale-like leaves
cones
usually keeps its leaves all year round

Deciduous or Broadleaf:
broad leaves
often has nuts, flowers, or fruit
loses its leaves each fall

Supplies
your science journal
pencil

2 Go outside to a place that has at least three trees, but more if possible. Look at each tree's branches carefully. Look at the ground around the tree. You will find some clues to help you decide whether the tree is a conifer or broadleaf. Write down your observations in your science journal.

Most oak trees don't grow **acorns** until they are at least 50 years old. If you plant an acorn, how old will you be before you can plant your tree's acorns?

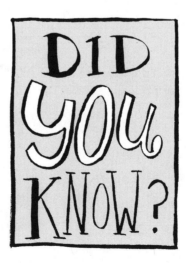
DID you KNOW?

Believe it or not, **palm trees** aren't actually trees. They are a type of flowering plant. More than 2,600 different kinds of palms live all over the world in tropical locations.

Things to notice

✿ Does the tree have needle-like or broad leaves?

✿ Are the branches full of leaves or leaf buds?

✿ Are there cones on the tree?

✿ Are there nuts or cones or other fruits on the ground near the tree?

✿ Can you draw a picture of the leaves?

✿ Can you draw a picture of the tree as you see it?

✿ How many of each kind of tree did you find?

✿ Are there more conifers or more broadleaf trees?

✿ Which kind of tree is bigger?

✿ Where might you go to look for the biggest broadleaf trees?

✿ Where might you find the biggest conifers?

Bamboo is a grass that grows in tropical climates, and it grows really fast—up to 3 feet in one day! Think about how long it would take you to grow 3 feet.

33

Sweet Sap Surprise

Some trees, like sugar maples, have very sweet sap in the spring. It's so sweet that people drill small holes in the maple trees and collect the sap in buckets to make maple syrup.

A fully grown maple tree can give up to 20 gallons of sap a day. This sounds like a lot, doesn't it? But to make maple syrup you boil the sap for hours and hours so that most of the liquid evaporates. You have to boil 40 gallons of sap to get one gallon of maple syrup.

Most kids have tasted maple syrup before, but did you know that some birch trees also have a familiar taste? If you cut off a small twig of a yellow birch tree in the spring and chew a bit on the twig, you'll taste spearmint!

The Rise of Sap

All trees have sap in them, which is a liquid that helps them grow new leaves and branches. In the winter, when the trees are **dormant**, the sap in deciduous trees remains quite still. When spring brings longer days, and the air and soil grow warm again, the sap begins to flow and the trees "wake up." Once the tree wakes up it begins to take in a lot of water through capillary action and new leaves grow. Remember what capillary action is? It's the process plants use to drink water. Fully grown trees can pull up to 40 gallons of water a day from the ground into their roots. Some of that water is released through the tree's leaves.

Pushing Buds

Why do trees seem to "pop" with leaves after a few days of warm rain in the spring? Because trees that bloom in the spring get ready in the late summer and fall. They grow the beginnings of new leaves on their branches in the fall, before they become dormant for the winter. In spring, when the soil has warmed and melted enough for tree roots to pull water from it, the tree buds finally get the water they need and POP open! Here's a way for you to see this for yourself.

1 Fill the vase with water. Place the twigs in the vase.

2 Check on the twigs at the same time each day. Keep the vase filled with water.

3 Sketch the buds in your science journal as they change.

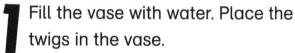

Things to notice

✿ How long did it take for the buds to open?

✿ Did all the buds open at the same time?

✿ How many days did it take for the twig to grow leaves?

✿ Did the twigs suck up the water in the vase? How much?

Supplies

vase

water

small branches cut from a willow or fruit tree

your science journal

Bark, Bark!

You may think that all trees look pretty much the same, especially in early spring when their leaves aren't quite out yet. But just like people, no two trees are exactly alike. Trees of the same family (or **species**) look a lot alike, but you can see they are not the same by looking at their bark.

A tree's bark protects it from disease and insects. It is like skin, or a suit of armor for the tree. When trees are young, their bark is smooth. As the trees grow older and bigger, their bark gets rougher. The only tree in North America that has bark that stays quite smooth when it grows is the beech tree.

Different North American trees have very different kinds of bark. Ash trees have bark that has a diamond pattern in it. Black cherry trees have bark that looks like potato chips layered on top of each other. Birch and sycamore trees have bark like paper that looks a bit shredded and peels off in layers. Birch bark has been used to make canoes, baskets, shoes, paper—even clothing!

Buzzz

Be a Bark Detective

This activity will help you learn to recognize different types of trees in early spring before you can rely on looking at their leaves. You will notice—or observe—what is similar and different about their bark. It's fun to be a bark detective!

1 Use your science journal to record the following information for each tree: What does the bark look like? What does the bark feel like? Does the tree bark have any special marks on it? What are they? Does the tree bark have any insects or animals on it?

2 Use your tree identification guide to identify each tree by its bark.

Things to notice

✿ Were any of the trees the same kind of tree?

✿ Do the trees have some things about their bark that are the same? Some things that are different?

✿ What are some ways that you can tell the difference between one tree's bark and another tree's bark?

Supplies

three trees of a similar size

pencil

your science journal

tree identification guide

The World's Largest and Oldest Trees!

Trees are the longest living organisms on earth. They are also the largest living thing.

The world's largest tree is a sequoia in California named General Sherman. A sequoia is a kind of redwood. General Sherman is more than 2,000 years old! It is 30 feet around and 275 feet tall. That is so big that you could fit your whole house inside of it!

The General Sherman tree isn't the oldest tree in the world, though. It is young compared to the Methuselah Tree. The Methuselah Tree is a kind of pine tree that also grows in California. The exact location is kept secret so no one cuts it down. Amazingly, this tree has been growing for almost 5,000 years. That means the Methuselah Tree was around when the Great Pyramids of Egypt were being built. And it's still growing today! Now THAT is an old tree!

wow!

Just for laughs

Q: What did the tree wear to the pool party?

A: Swimming trunks!

How Old Is That Tree?

Just like plants, trees grow fastest in the spring because there is more sunlight, more water, and warmer air. You can count how old a tree was when it was cut down by counting the number of rings in the stump. Usually the tree will have thin, darker rings, and wider, lighter rings. Those wider, lighter rings are from spring growth. But how do you figure out how old a tree is when it is still standing tall? This activity will give you a rough idea how old a tree is. This method works best on softwood or fast-growing trees, such as birch, beech, and ash. It doesn't work for all trees, especially maple, oak, and other slow-growing hardwood trees.

1 Measure a spot on the tree trunk about 5 feet from the ground. Wrap the measuring tape around the tree at that spot.

2 Each inch around represents about a year in the age of a tree. For example, if the tree measures 20 inches around, the tree is about 20 years old.

Supplies
tree
measuring tape
pencil
your science journal

39

Make Your Own Paper

Did you know that paper comes from trees? In this activity you'll make your own paper using recycled material, and you'll add some pieces of tree leaves and bark to it! This is a messy activity that might seem a little complicated at first, but it is easy and lots of fun.

1 Tear the scrap paper into 1-inch pieces. Soak the torn paper pieces in warm water in one of the large tubs for at least 30 minutes. You can soak them overnight.

2 Bend the wire hanger to make a square-shaped frame. It should be smaller than the opening of the tub. Cover the hanger with the old nylon stocking. Staple the stocking in place to make a screen.

3 Fill the blender halfway with warm water. Add a handful of the soaked paper. Make sure the lid is on tight! Blend at a medium speed until you can't see the pieces of paper. It will look like paper soup. This is paper pulp.

4 Pour the blended mixture into the other big tub or pot. Stir in pieces of tree bark, leaves, or flowers.

5 Pour warm water over the mixture so it is completely covered. Mix it all together really well.

6 Slide the wire frame into the big tub and let some of the paper pulp settle on the screen. Hold the frame underwater and gently move it back and forth to get an even layer of pulp on the screen, then lift it out of the water.

Supplies

5 pieces of scrap paper like paper towels, construction paper, and tissue paper

2 large tubs or pots

warm water

wire clothes hanger

old nylon stocking

stapler

blender

pieces of tree bark, leaves, flower petals, thread, or string

sponge

dishtowels or plain newsprint (for blotting)

rolling pin

household iron

strainer

7 Let the frame drip over the tub until most of the water has drained through the screen. You should have an even layer of paper pulp on the screen. Press the pulp gently with your hand to squeeze out extra water. You can soak up the extra water from the bottom of the screen with a sponge.

8 Place the clean dishtowels or plain newsprint on a flat surface. Flip the screen so the paper side is down. Lift off the screen really gently. The paper will be on the newsprint.

9 Cover the paper with another dishcloth or piece of newsprint and squeeze out any extra water by rolling over it with a rolling pin. Make as many sheets of paper as you like this way. Let them dry overnight.

10 When the paper is almost dry you can ask a grownup to help you iron it to make it completely dry. The iron will help smooth it out, too. When the paper is all dry, you can very gently pull off the dishcloth or newsprint from both ends. This will stretch it so the paper will come off without tearing.

Just for laughs

Q: What did the beaver say to the tree?

A: It's been nice gnawing you!

Caution

When you are done making paper, collect the leftover pulp in a strainer and throw it out. Don't put it down the drain or you will clog the pipes!

Animals on the Move

Spring is a time when the animal world is on the move. Many animals travel to a certain place for the winter months, then travel back again to their homes in the spring.

This is called **migration**. Migration is different from just traveling because the animal goes back to the same place every year at around the same time.

43

Animals are not taught by their parents how to migrate.

Let's go!

They are born knowing how to do it.

This built in understanding is called instinct.

One instinct humans have from the moment they are born is the urge to cry to communicate.

Can you think of other instincts humans have?

Some animals migrate to warmer places when winter comes because colder weather means their food supply gets low. Other animals need to migrate because their bodies are not able to handle the cold of winter. In the spring, when the weather gets warmer and there is more food to eat, these animals return to their summer homes and have babies.

Animals that migrate know when to get ready to migrate by **instinct**. Scientists think that the sun tells them when it is time to get ready to travel in fall and spring. When summer days get shorter, animals know it is time to travel to their winter homes. When the winter days grow longer, animals know it is time to get ready for their journey to their summer homes.

Just for laughs

Q: Why do seagulls fly over the sea and not the bay?

A: They don't want to be called bagels!

Why Do Animals Migrate Back North?

If birds and animals migrate south in the fall because there is more food and nice weather, why do they come back north again? Why not stay where they are and save all that time going back and forth? Because the seasons change everywhere, even in the tropics. These changes affect food and shelter, too. Monarch butterflies winter in the tropical mountains of Mexico, but they need to eat milkweed, which only grows in more northern climates during the summer months. Lots of birds migrate to the tropics in the fall, but come back in the spring because the rainy season in the tropics affects the food supply there. They fly back to the north in the spring when there is a lot of food there and the weather is warm.

These Animals All Migrate

You probably know that many different kinds of birds, like geese, migrate north in the spring. But did you know that all different kinds of animals migrate? Whales, seals, manatees, elk, moose, deer, butterflies, crabs and lobsters, some kinds of fish, turtles and frogs, and even bats migrate each year. Some migrate only a very short distance, like frogs. Others migrate quite far. The sooty shearwater is a seabird that migrates 6,000 miles each spring, from New Zealand to California.

45

Who Is the Early Bird?

Birds are often the first animals to migrate in the spring. In this activity you will keep track of the dates when you first hear or see different spring birds! Remember that many birds live where you do all year round. But what are some birds that leave in the fall and come back in the spring? You can learn more about what kinds of local birds migrate at www.audubon.org. You can also ask a grownup to suggest a local bird.

1 Choose a bird that you know migrates in the spring to where you live. Research the color and song of the bird. Draw a picture of the bird in your science journal.

2 Birds are most active in the early morning and early evening. Go outside and listen and look for your bird. The first time you see your bird, write down the date and time in your science journal.

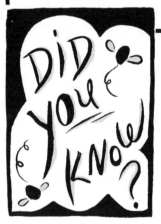

Sea creatures such as seals and whales use **echolocation** to figure out where they are going. Can you guess from the parts of this word— echo and location—what these creatures

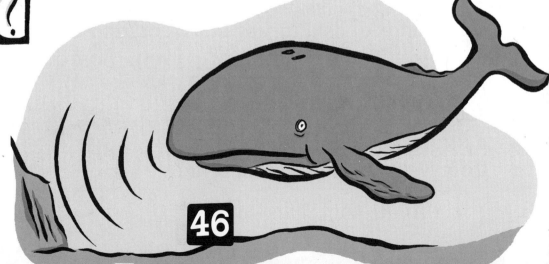

Things to notice

✿ Was the bird you chose the first bird you saw or heard in the spring?

✿ If not, do you know what bird was the first one?

are doing? They send out sound waves that bounce off objects, or echo, to keep them on track. The cool thing about echolocation is that the animals can use it any time they travel, not just when they migrate.

Words 2 Know

migration: annual movement of groups of animals from one region to another for feeding or breeding.

instinct: an inherited, natural pattern of behavior.

migratory bird: a bird that migrates.

flyway: air route used by migrating birds.

How Do Animals Know Where to Go?

Some animals migrate very long distances. How do they know where to go? Animals have different ways of finding their way.

Some scientists think birds and butterflies use the sun and stars to guide their way. Other scientists believe that they are able to use the earth's magnetic field to help them get where they need to go. Scientists have discovered that some kinds of night-flying birds get lost when flying in heavy fog, but not when the nights are clear. That's why scientists think these birds use the stars to keep track of where they are going.

Other scientists have studied butterfly migration. They think that somehow butterflies use the sun as a kind of compass, keeping them on track.

48

A bird that migrates is called a **migratory bird**. Most migratory birds in North America travel along **flyways**. These are very large north–south air routes used by thousands and thousands of birds to migrate. It's like a giant highway in the sky for birds.

There are four major flyways in North America. These flyways have names: the Atlantic, Pacific, central, and Mississippi flyways. Different groups of birds fly in different parts of the flyways, called corridors. In a way, these corridors are a bit like the lanes on a highway, but on a very, very, very big highway!

Land and sea animals also have migration routes that they use over and over again. Some mammals, such as deer, elk, and moose use paths that other animals have used before them, and they smell their way back each year. Other animals use landmarks, which are places that they remember. This way they make sure they are going the right way. Scientists think whales and other migratory sea animals look for and remember certain landmarks when they are migrating up and down the coastlines.

How Far Can You Go?

Why do some animals travel very far each spring, and some stay so close to home? This activity will help you think about why different kinds of animals travel different distances when they migrate. For this activity you will need a few people: one to call out animal names, and the others to be migrating animals.

1 Make a list of animals that move in different ways. You can include a bird that flies, a snake that slithers, a lobster that crawls backwards, and a deer that runs.

2 Decide how a human can best imitate how each of the animals on your list moves. Have everyone practice moving like each of the different animals.

3 Mark a starting point. This mark is the winter home of your animal, and where the racers will start their spring migration.

4 Measure about 25 meters or yards from the starting point. Mark that point. That is the finish line, and the summer home of your animal.

Supplies

list of migrating animals

measuring tape

an open area like a hallway, playground, or your back yard

5 Choose someone to be the caller. They will call out "ready, set," and then the name of a migrating animal instead of "go."

6 The racers must then begin migrating from the start to the finish using that animal's form of movement. If you are a goose, you can fly. If you are a snake, you must slither. If you are a whale, you must swim. If you are a lobster, you must crawl. If you are a deer, you can run or walk. While the racers are migrating, the caller can shout out a new animal, and the racers all change how they move to match that new animal.

7 Another fun variation on this activity is to use a stopwatch to time how long it takes each animal to migrate from its winter home to its summer home.

Things to notice

❀ Which animals were able to move fastest?

❀ Which animals were slowest?

❀ Is migration easy for all animals?

❀ What affects how far an animal can migrate?

The Amazing Monarch Butterfly

The monarch butterfly is an amazing creature. It is a large, orange-and-black-speckled butterfly that lives everywhere in North America except for the Pacific Northwest. You won't find a monarch butterfly in the states of Oregon and Washington, or in Vancouver, but they live pretty much everywhere else.

Each year, monarch butterflies migrate thousands of miles. In the fall, monarchs in the north gather into a large group and begin to fly south together. They travel from almost everywhere in North America towards their winter homes in Mexico and California.

In the spring, the monarchs fly back to their summer homes in the north. But most monarchs can't make the whole journey back. They die on the way, before they make it to their summer homes. Before they die, the butterflies lay eggs, which hatch and turn to caterpillars. The caterpillars eat milkweed plants and grow until they spin a cocoon around themselves. When the cocoon splits open, a new monarch butterfly comes out.

That monarch butterfly continues on the journey north to the same place the parent monarch was going, even though it has never been there before! In the fall, that same monarch flies south, all the way to Mexico, even though it has never been there before. Isn't that amazing?

Make Your Own
Butterfly Caterpillar Fan

1 Color the butterfly and caterpillar templates, which you'll find at the back of the book. Lay the caterpillar template over the butterfly template, and line up the edges of the paper.

2 Cut the paper into even strips. Line up the strips in order, alternating between butterfly strips and caterpillar strips.

3 Glue the strips onto the construction paper as you lined them up. After the glue has dried, fold the construction paper like an accordion.

4 Unfold the paper and hold it like a fan. Look at your fan from one side and you will see a butterfly. Look at your fan from the other angle and you will see a caterpillar.

Things to notice

✿ What is similar about a monarch butterfly and a monarch butterfly caterpillar?

Supplies

butterfly and caterpillar templates

colored pencils or crayons

scissors

large piece of construction paper, 8 by 14 inches

glue stick

Amazing

After bees, butterflies are the second largest group of pollinators.

A butterfly can fly up to 12 miles per hour.

Butterflies live on all the continents around the world except Antarctica, where it is too cold.

Butterfly

Butterflies cannot fly if their body temperature is less than 86 degrees.

Butterflies fly during the day, while moths generally fly at night.

A caterpillar grows to about 27,000 times the size it was when it first emerged from its egg. If a human baby that weighed 9 pounds at birth grew at the same rate as a caterpillar, it would weigh 243,000 pounds when fully grown. Rather large!

Facts

Butterflies rest with their wings closed. This is the opposite of moths, who rest with their wings open. People who study or collect butterflies are called "lepidopterists."

Spring is for Babies!

Chapter 5

Spring is a time when lots of animal babies are born. Why? Because the weather is warm. There is plenty of food to eat.

And new babies have the whole summer to grow and learn how to survive before the cold, hard winter sets in. If babies were born in the summer or fall, they would still be very young when the weather turned colder. It would be much harder for them to survive the chilly fall and winter. Spring is the best time for having babies in the wild.

Finding & Making Homes

Animals have homes just like people do. Many animals make new homes in the spring. Their homes aren't quite like ours (they probably don't have a TV or microwave oven!), but animals have homes for the same reasons we do. They need a place to have their babies and keep their families safe from danger and bad weather.

Animals are born knowing what kind of home they need. This is another instinct. Some animals find simple shelters to call home. Other animals build very complicated structures. And some use homes that other animals built before them. They just move right on in and make themselves comfortable!

Animal Babies Live in These Homes

A dove lives
in a cote

A chicken
lives in a coop

A bird lives
in a nest

A bee live
in a hiv

56

Spring is for Babies!

Most animals build their homes using natural materials like grass, dirt, sticks, and mud. It all depends on the kind of home they need, and where they live. Animals that live on or near the ground will make or find homes close to the ground. Some **mammals**, like skunks, rabbits, chipmunks, and groundhogs dig burrows underground to have their babies. Often snakes will find old burrows and make them into their homes. Sometimes the old owners come back to find a new animal has moved in!

An eagle lives in an aerie

Wild bees and wasps live in a byke

A baby kangaroo lives in a pouch

A fox lives in a den or earth

An otter lives in a holt

A beaver lives in a lodge

A bat lives in a roost

A badger lives in a sett or earth

57

Some animals make their homes using material they make from their own bodies. Many insects do this. Bees make their own homes from beeswax, which comes from their bodies. Paper wasps build nests using their own spit, which hardens into a soft, paper-like material. Spiders spin webs from their own silk.

Large animals like deer and moose don't build homes. These kinds of animals move around a lot, so they have their babies in the woods or in tall grass. They push some grass down into a soft nest for their baby, but leave tall grass all around so the nest is hidden.

Animals that live in trees, like squirrels, make nests in high places. They sometimes find holes in trees to make their nests in. Squirrels will also make big nests of leaves and twigs in the crook of a tree, or will even make a nest in a human house!

It takes a song bird about six days to build a nest.

It takes three days to build the outside, and three more on the inside.

The material used to make the inside of the nest is usually much softer than the outside.

Birds Sing More in Spring

Have you ever noticed that the birds make more noise in spring than at any other time of year? It's true! Birds sing more in the spring because they are trying to find mates. Male birds sing loudly to tell other male birds that this territory is off limits to them. Male birds also sing to attract female birds, who sing back.

Ask your mom and dad if they have any stories of animals nesting in the house—they may have some good ones.

Animals like coyotes, foxes, and wolves make dens. Sometimes they dig their dens in the ground. Other times they will find a small space in a cave, or at the bottom of a tree. When their babies are a little older, these animals move out of their dens and spend most of their time outdoors.

It's not easy to find an animal's home. That's because animals try to keep their homes hidden. They want to keep their babies out of sight, so they spend a lot of time finding the safest, hardest-to-find place for their homes that they can.

Words 2 Know

mammals: animals that make milk for their babies.

predators: animals that hunt and eat other animals.

fledglings: baby birds that are learning to fly.

camouflage: how the way an animal looks helps it to blend in with its surroundings.

59

What's Best for a Nest?

Birds build their nests out of lots of different kinds of material. You can find birds' nests made of twigs, straw, grass, even ribbons or thread a bird might find on the ground.

Where do they find all their nest-building materials? This activity will explore what kinds of materials birds might choose to build their nests, and how far away they might go to find the material.

1 Choose four different places in your yard. Take one piece of yarn and one piece of ribbon and place them in each of the four spots. Try to put the yarn and ribbon at different heights: one or two on a tree branch or on a bush, and one or two on the ground.

2 Write down in your science journal where you put each piece of yarn and ribbon. Each day go outside to check if the yarn and ribbon have been taken.

Supplies

4 pieces of yarn or string: 2 of one color and 2 of another color

4 pieces of ribbon or thread: 2 of one color and 2 of another color

your science journal

pencil

60

3 Write down in your science journal which pieces of yarn or ribbon are gone, and from which locations.

Things to notice

❀ Did the birds like one color more than another?

❀ Did the birds like one material more than another?

❀ Did it matter how high you put the thread?

❀ Which height did the birds like best for materials?

❀ Did you notice any of your materials in a nearby nest?

Other things to think about

❀ Have you ever found a bird's nest or other animal's home? What did you notice about it?

❀ Where did you find it? Was it well hidden?

❀ What kind of animal built it? How did you know?

Build a Bird's Nest

Building a nest in a tree can be tricky. The nest has to be strong so it can hold eggs and the bird who sits on them. The nest has to be stable so a strong wind or storm won't blow it out of the tree. And the nest has to be warm so the new chicks stay safe and protected when they hatch. And remember, birds can only use their beaks to build it.

In this activity you will see how hard it is to build a strong, safe nest. Try to build the strongest nest you can out of the fewest materials. You will start out with only a few materials and see how many pennies your nest can hold without collapsing or dropping the pennies through the nest. Then you will add material to make the nest stronger. To be even more like a bird, try using only two fingers to make your nest!

Supplies

3 small branches or 3 rulers

30 strips of 1/2-inch-wide paper

30 toothpicks

10 pieces of 3-inch thread or dental floss

10 pieces of 2-inch pipe cleaner

pennies

you science journal

1 Make a nesting platform out of the branches or rulers by making a triangle. This is where you will build your nest.

2 Start with 10 strips of paper, 10 toothpicks, 3 pieces of thread, and 3 pieces of pipe cleaner. Arrange these materials in the way you think will make the best nest.

3 When you are ready, put pennies in the nest. How many pennies can you add before they fall through the bottom? Write down the materials you used and the number of pennies your nest held.

4 Try building your nest again using all the materials. Can you think of a better way to arrange the materials the second time? Record your observations.

Things to notice

✿ What was the hardest part about building a nest?

✿ Did some material work better than others?

✿ Did some material work better in different places?

✿ Was it hard to only use two fingers to build your nest?

✿ What else did you notice?

How Animal Babies Stay Safe

Human mothers almost never leave their babies alone, but animal mothers do all the time. Animal babies are actually safer left alone than with their mothers all the time. Many animal babies have no scent, so other animals can't smell them. When the babies are alone and hidden, they are safe from **predators**. A predator is an animal that hunts and eats other animals. Predators can find adult animals easily because adult animals have a scent. If a baby stays with its mother, it might be discovered by the predator, too.

Animal parents often leave their babies alone during the day. Deer and rabbits only visit their babies once or twice a day to nurse them. The rest of the day the mothers are close by, but not

Why are Bird Nests Easy to Find?

Birds make nests that are often easy for humans to see. Most birds build their nests in trees. Trees make a safe place for bird nests, because most animals can't climb trees to reach the eggs. We can see them more easily than other animals can because we walk upright. Most animals walk on four legs and are much closer to the ground, so they can't see nests in trees as easily as we can.

Colors Are Also Warnings

Sometimes baby animals have colors that don't help them blend in to their surroundings, but make them stand out. One kind of amphibian, called a red-spotted newt, has babies that are bright, orange–red. The babies are called red efts. Their bright color is a warning to other animals that their skin is poisonous. When the red eft grows into an adult newt, it changes color to a brown–green.

right near their babies. This keeps the babies safe from any predators that are hunting.

Baby birds that are learning to fly are called **fledglings**. They are often on the ground by themselves. But if you look around, you will probably see a mother bird in a tree, watching over her baby. She will bring food to the fledgling every 20 minutes or so.

Baby animals have other ways to stay safe from predators. One way is how they look. Many animal babies have fur or feathers that are a different color than their parents. A baby fawn, for example, has light-colored spots on its brown coat. Adult deer don't have spots on their brown coats. The light spots help the fawn blend into wherever it is hidden. This is called **camouflage**. Camouflage is how an animal's appearance helps it to blend in with its surroundings. Baby birds are usually grayish-brown, no matter what color their parents are. Their drab colors blend in with their nests so it's hard for predators to see them.

Camouflage Treasure

It's hard to find baby animals in the wild, because they blend in so well with their surroundings. Here's a way you can see for yourself how hard it is to find something that looks like everything around it. You'll need two people for this activity—one to hide the shapes and the other to hunt for them.

1 Cut out the following shapes from the pieces of your construction paper. It doesn't matter what colors you use for your shapes.

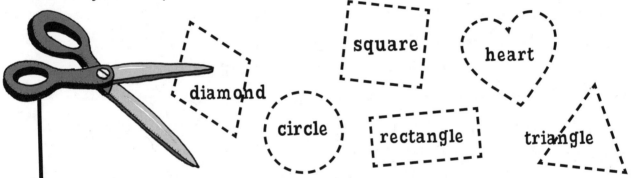

2 Have one person hide the shapes around your house. That person should try to put the shapes on things that have the same colors or patterns as the shape. For example, hide the white shape in a white bathtub. Hide a black shape on a black stove, and a red rectangle shape on a red-striped chair, etc. While that person is hiding shapes, the other person CANNOT peek. See how long it takes the other person to find all the shapes.

Supplies

scissors

pieces of construction paper in 4 or 5 different colors that are the same colors as things in your house

Hunt

3 Now have one person hide the shapes around your house in places that DON'T have the same colors or patterns. Again, don't let the person who will be searching for the shapes peek. For example, hide the white shape on the black stove, and the black shape on a red-striped chair, etc. Now see how long it takes the other person to find all the shapes.

Things to notice

❀ Was it easier to find the shapes the second time around? Why?

❀ Which pieces were hardest to find and why?

❀ Did shape or color matter more when you tried to find the pieces?

❀ What else did you notice?

What's in a Name?

Baby animals have special names. Here are a few:

Bear—cub
Beaver—kit
Bird—fledgling
Cat—kitten
Cow—calf
Deer—fawn, yearling
Dog—pup, puppy
Duck—duckling
Eagle—eaglet
Elephant—calf
Elephant seal—weaner
Fish—fry
Fowl—chick, chicken
Fox—cub, pup
Frog—polliwog, tadpole
Goat—kid
Goose—gosling
Grouse—cheeper
Hawk—eyas
Hen—pullet
Hippo—calf

Horse—foal, yearling, colt (male), filly (female)
Kangaroo—joey
Lion—cub
Owl—owlet
Partridge—cheeper
Pig—piglet, shoat, farrow, suckling
Pigeon—squab, squeaker
Quail—cheeper
Rabbit—bunny, kit
Rat—pup
Rhino—calf
Rooster—cockerel
Salmon—parr, smolt
Seal—pup
Sheep—lamb
Swan—cygnet
Tiger—cub, whelp
Turkey—poult
Whale—calf
Zebra—foal

WOW! Most baby birds learn to fly when they are between 2 weeks and a month old.

Just for laughs

Q: What is a baby bee?

A: A little humbug!

See a Baby Animal? Leave It Alone!

If you are outside in the spring you might see baby animals by themselves. Baby animals might look like they are lost, but their mothers are usually close by. They will not come near their babies until the baby is alone again. A baby bird that has all of its feathers and is hopping around is learning how to fly. Its parents will be close by.

Animal Babies Grow Fast

When animal babies are born in the spring, they grow quickly—usually much quicker than human babies do. Why is that? Because most animals can't find lots of food all year round. Humans can go to the grocery store any time during the year to restock their cupboards, but animals can't do this. Animals that migrate have to grow quickly enough to be ready to travel by the end of the summer. Animals that don't migrate have to grow strong and healthy to get ready for the change from summer to winter.

In fall and winter, food is often harder to find. Weak animals can get sick and die. That is another reason why it is important that animal babies grow quickly after they are born. When baby deer are born they weigh about the same as a newborn human baby—about 6 or 7 pounds. But fawns grow much faster than a human baby does. Fawns stop nursing, lose their spots, and look just like adult deer when they are only four months old. And when they are six months old, fawns are ready to live on their own. They weigh between 65 and 90 pounds. Human babies are usually just learning how to sit up by themselves when they are 6 months old, and they might weigh only about 18 pounds.

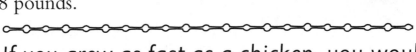

If you grew as fast as a chicken, you would be HUGE! Chicks grow about 3 pounds per month. But they start out at only a few ounces. If you grew at the same rate a baby chicken does, you'd weigh 2,835 pounds by the time you were 2 years old.

Mammals that only eat meat give birth only one time a year. Mammals that eat plants often give birth two or more times in the spring and summer.

Just for laughs

Q: What did one egg say to the other egg?

A: Let's get cracking!

What Do Baby Animals Eat?

What a baby animal eats depends on what kind of animal it is. Mammal babies drink milk from their mothers until they are old enough to eat solid food. Baby birds are fed by their parents, too. Birds can't bring a lot of food to their babies at one time unless they carry the food in their stomachs—so that's what they do. They eat as much as they can, then fly back to their nest and spit up some partially digested food for their babies. Baby frogs, called tadpoles, eat algae and other pond plants, and sometimes worms and even other tadpoles! Some creatures, such as snakes and lizards, don't have special baby diets—they are born ready to eat whatever food adults eat.

Babies Grow Fast!

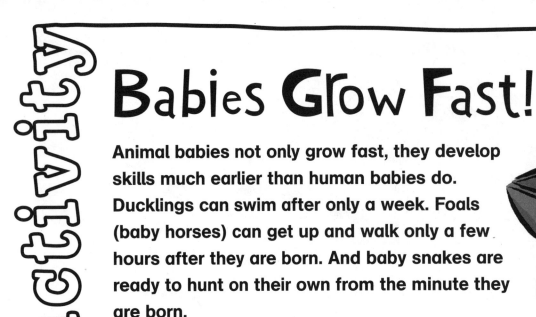

Animal babies not only grow fast, they develop skills much earlier than human babies do. Ducklings can swim after only a week. Foals (baby horses) can get up and walk only a few hours after they are born. And baby snakes are ready to hunt on their own from the minute they are born.

Why? Because unlike human babies, animal babies need to be ready to survive on their own at a very young age. This is usually well before they turn a year old. Humans are usually taken care of by their parents until they are teenagers—or even older. That's years and years! In this activity you will do some research to see at what age you achieve some important milestones that animals also achieve. You can ask your parents, teachers, or other family friends or relatives. Your parents may have a book where they wrote down when you first managed these accomplishments.

Answer the following questions:

✿ At what age did you sit up by yourself?
✿ At what age did you stand up by yourself?
✿ At what age did you begin to walk?
✿ At what age did you say your first word?
✿ At what age did you learn to feed yourself?
✿ At what age did you learn to swim?

Supplies

your science journal

pencil

Spring Weather

Spring is the time of year when the weather is hardest to predict. Why? It has to do with the way the air and sun work together.

The earth is a very big place, and all of it is surrounded by air. The air moves around all the time, all over the earth. And it is always trying to make the temperature the same everywhere. That is definitely not an easy thing to do.

Remember how the sun's rays hit the Northern Hemisphere at an angle during the winter? That means the sun is lower in the sky, and so the earth doesn't get as much of the sun's light or heat. That causes the oceans and land to cool down. In some places the land and water freeze solid. Then in the spring, the sun appears higher and higher in the sky. Its rays hit the earth more directly and make the air warm right up. But the ground takes longer to warm up. It is still cold from winter, and in northern places there is still snow on the ground. The ocean is also still very cold because

Just for laughs

Q: What happens when it rains cats and dogs?

A: You have to be careful not to step in a poodle.

Words 2 Know

atmosphere: all of the air around the earth.

convection: the upward or downward movement of warm and cool air that forms many clouds.

What is weather?

Weather is not something that happens just when clouds arrive, or when the wind blows, or when it rains or snows. The weather is what our **atmosphere**—the air around the earth—is doing all the time. Sunny skies, little puffs of wind, no rain for a week—that is weather. It is just as much weather as a howling rain storm. But there is no question, the more powerful the weather is, the more we pay attention to it.

it takes a long time to warm up so much water.

So in spring, the air and sun have a lot more work to do to even out the temperatures. The warm air that is heated by the sun and the cold air coming from the frozen ground can bump up against each other. That means the weather changes from warm to cold, and back again. These changes help clouds to grow very quickly. Sometimes spring storms have such large clouds that they make lots of rain, and sometimes lightning, hail, and even tornadoes. But remember the warm air and the cold air are close together. The weather can change from sunny and warm to snowy and cold in just a few hours. Spring weather can be crazy!

There are three main types of clouds

cumulus clouds—puffy clouds that look like puffs of cotton and are often a sign of fair weather

stratus clouds—flat sheets of clouds that are often a sign of stormy weather

cirrus clouds—high curly, feathery clouds that are often a sign of fair weather

Clouds

Look up! Spring is a great time for cloud watching. Clouds are collections of tiny water droplets. Clouds are formed when the warm air that is being heated by the strong, spring sun rays meets the cold, damp air coming up off of the cold ground. Little water drops form into clouds. The water drops are so small and light that they can float in the air. When enough water droplets have gathered together, they get too heavy to float and fall down as rain. There are lots of clouds in spring because the sun's rays are strong and the ground is still quite chilly.

Fog is a cloud, too, that lies very close to the ground. There is often a lot of fog in the spring. Fog forms when rising warm, wet air meets sinking cold air and condenses into water droplets. It happens a lot in spring because the water that has been frozen in the earth is warmed and melted by the sun's strong rays. At night, the air temperature goes down, the cold air sinks, and the warm air from the melting frost meets the cold air. The result: fog!

Make Your Own Cloud

How do clouds form when warm air and cold air meet? Here is a way you can see up close! In this project you will be using both hot water and a match, so you'll need a grownup's help.

1 Tape the piece of black paper around the bottom half of the jar. Fill the jar to the top with hot water. Leave it for about a minute. Then pour out all but an inch of the water.

2 Have an adult light the match and hold it over the jar opening for a few seconds. Drop the match in the water. Then quickly put the plastic bag of ice cubes over the top of the jar.

3 What happened? The warm water and the match heated the air inside the jar. The warm, wet air rose up to the top of the jar and ran into the cold air just below the ice cubes. When the warm, wet air met the cold wet air, they created a cloud of water droplets.

Things to notice

✿ What happened to the air in the jar?

✿ What did the ice cubes do?

✿ What else did you notice?

Supplies

glass jar

piece of black paper cut to fit halfway up around the jar

tape

hot tap water

match

ice cubes in a plastic bag

Spring Is For Thunderstorms— and Sometimes Tornadoes

In many parts of the country, spring time means thunderstorm time. That's because thunderstorms happen when lots of cold air meets lots of warm, damp air. The two kinds of air meet and move around each other. This is called **convection**. Convection makes clouds grow. As the clouds grow, they tumble together, and rise and collect with water. Those big, warm, water-filled clouds get pushed up higher and higher into the sky, where they meet more cold air. The energy created by the very warm and the very cold air moving around together causes lightning and thunder.

Sometimes, the difference between the warm air and cold air can make so much energy that the air begins to spin around itself like a top. When this happens, a cloud shaped like a funnel can form. A funnel cloud that comes out of the sky and touches the ground is called a tornado. A funnel cloud can occur anywhere, but most tornados happen in places where there is lots of open farmland. Why? Because tornados need moisture to grow, and in the spring, the warm, wet soil of farmland helps create lots of warm, wet air to feed the thunderstorms that cause tornadoes.

Make Your Own Thunderstorm

How do thunderstorms form? It can be a little tricky to understand. But here's a way to see for yourself how convection (warm air meeting cold air) works to create a storm. In this experiment, the blue ice cubes are cold air and the red water is warm air. Watch what happens when they meet.

1 Fill the ice cube tray with water. Add blue food coloring to the water. Freeze until solid.

2 Fill the plastic container a little more than halfway full with warm (not hot) water. Place a blue ice cube at one end of the plastic container. Then add three drops of red food coloring to the water at the other end of the plastic container.

Things to Notice

✿ What happened to the ice cube in the warm water?

✿ What happened to the drops of red food coloring?

✿ What else did you notice?

DID YOU KNOW?

Tornadoes happen all over the world, but the places that get the most tornadoes are Kansas, Oklahoma, and Missouri. That's why this area of the United States is known as "tornado alley."

Supplies
ice cube tray

blue food coloring

warm water

clear, plastic container the size of a shoebox

red food coloring

Make Some Thunder

Have you ever been scared by a loud clap of thunder? Thunder is just the sound that lightning makes when it heats up the air around it. The lightning's energy is so strong that is sends out a shock wave of sound—that's thunder. It's a little bit like what happens when you throw a rock into a puddle. The rock hits the water and sends out ripples of waves. Thunder is the same thing, except with sound. This is an easy way to show how lightning's quick release of energy makes a loud sound wave.

1 Blow up your lunch bag and twist the neck tightly shut. Now quickly pop the bag with both hands. Your hands are the power of lightning. The force of your hands hitting the bag so hard squeezes the air so it bursts through the bag.

2 That's what lightning does—it releases energy through the air very, very quickly. The loud popping sound of the bag is the result of the wave of air popping through the paper, just like thunder is a wave of sound popping through the air.

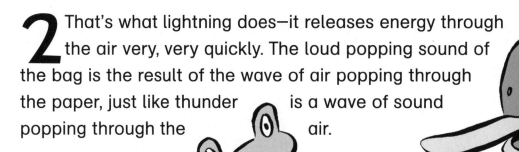

Supplies

brown paper
lunch bags

WOW! You can figure out how many miles away a thunderstorm is by doing some math. When you see lightning, count the number of seconds between the lightning strike and when you hear thunder. Take half of that number—this is the same as dividing by two. For example, if you count to four between when you see the lightning and hear the thunder, then your number is two. If you count to six, then your number is three. What does this tell you? How many miles away the storm is from you. Lightning and thunder happen at the same time, but sound travels much more slowly than light. If you can hear thunder right when lightning strikes, it means the storm is right on top of you!

Dark Clouds are Usually Storm Clouds

Most clouds look white because they reflect the light of the sun. If you see dark clouds, that means a storm is brewing. Dark clouds are dark because they are full of water droplets or ice crystals. If there is enough water or ice in a cloud, light can't shine through the cloud, which is why the cloud looks dark.

Wind

You might have noticed that spring days are often really windy, especially in the afternoon. You can thank the sun for that. The sun's rays are warming up the ground. That warm air rises, just like a hot air balloon. As it goes up, cooler air sinks to take its place.

Remember, the air in our atmosphere is always moving around, trying to make the temperature the same everywhere. Often the cooler air that is sinking down moves faster than the warm air that is rising up, because it doesn't have anything in its path, like trees or buildings, to slow it down. This results in gusty winds. In the mornings and at night, the winds tend to die down. That's because the sun hasn't heated the air close to the surface of the earth yet, so it isn't rising.

Just for laughs

Q: What did one raindrop say to the other raindrop?

A: My plop is bigger than your plop!

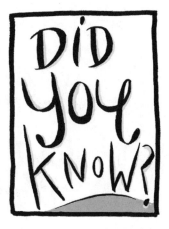

Raindrops range in size from $\frac{1}{100}$ inch to ¼ inch around. Rain falls in still air (not blown by the wind) about 7 to 18 miles an hour. That's pretty fast!

Spring Can Mean Floods

Spring is the time of year when floods are most likely to happen. Why? As the earth warms up, lots of water that has been frozen in the soil melts and rises to the surface. Since the ground warms up slowly, that water isn't absorbed back into the soil. It sits on top. That's why the ground is often so muddy in the spring. Some of this water makes its way to rivers and streams. As the sun's rays grow stronger and longer, frozen snow and ice on mountains begins to melt quickly, also coming down to rivers and making them higher than usual. On top of all this, you've just learned that spring time means lots of rain and storms. All that water falls into the rivers and streams, too. Sometimes there is just too much water for the river or streambed to hold. The water comes up over the river banks and floods everything around it.

Make a Wind Chime

Spring is known for its windy weather. In this project you will make a wind chime that you can hang outside to make some sunny spring wind music.

1 Use your scissors to cut six or seven pieces of fishing line. Make them all different lengths. If you don't have any fishing line handy you can also use string or twine, but remember that twine and string won't last as long outdoors.

2 Tie two pieces of fishing line that are the same length onto each end of the stick. You will use these to tie your wind chime to a post or tree.

3 Tie the remaining pieces of fishing line to several small metal objects. Then tie the other end of the fishing line to the stick. Try to space out each piece of fishing line about half an inch or an inch apart so the metal objects can swing easily but still hit each other when the wind blows on them.

4 Hang your wind chime from a tree branch and wait for a windy day.

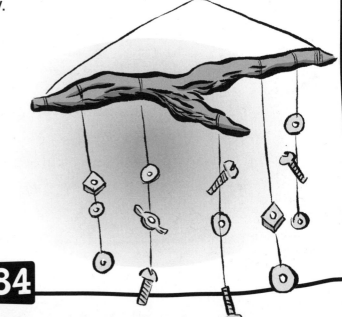

Supplies

fishing line

scissors

stick

small metal objects, such as washers, bolts, nuts, screws, and nails

tree branch

Conclusion

Did you enjoy learning about spring? Share what you've learned with others. They will be amazed! Not only is spring the busiest time of year, in most places it is a time of fantastic change. As spring days get longer and warmer, the earth wakes up from its winter nap. Plants grow, and the world greens right up. Animals come out of hibernation or migrate to their summer homes, and have babies. Insects start buzzing and whizzing through the air. Plants and animals and birds and bugs are busy, busy, busy. Meanwhile the weather can be very unpredictable. The weather can change so quickly in spring that you have to be ready for anything—maybe even snow!

As you share all of the amazing facts you've learned about spring with your family and friends, show them how to do your favorite experiments from the book, too. By exploring the outdoors and doing experiments from this book with others, you will help them discover the incredible ways that the world and its creatures survive and come back to life in spring. The more people know about the miracle of spring and the seasons, the more they will understand about how nature works. And learning about nature is the first step in making sure we protect it, so spread the word!

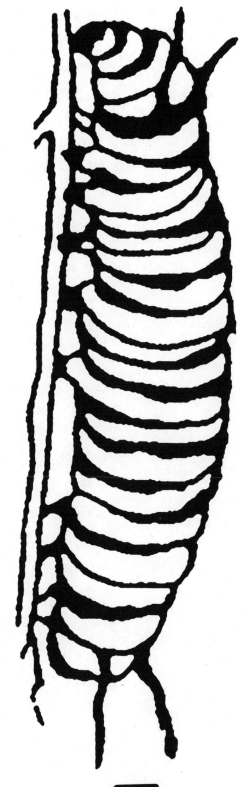

atmosphere: all of the air around the earth.

camouflage: how the way an animal looks helps it to blend in with its surroundings.

capillary action: the way plants pull water up from the soil into their leaves.

chlorophyll: the chemical inside plant leaves that helps them make food.

collect: to gather things to observe them.

conifer trees: trees that have cones and leaves like needles—most conifers are also evergreen trees.

convection: the upward or downward movement of warm and cool air that forms many clouds.

data: a collection of facts.

deciduous trees: trees that lose their leaves in the fall and grow new ones in the spring.

dormant: when plants are dormant they stop growing for a period of time.

equator: the imaginary line running around the middle of the earth that divides it in two halves.

equinox: two times a year when the earth has exactly 12 hours of daylight and 12 hours of night—March 22 and September 21.

evergreen trees: trees that don't lose their leaves in the fall and stay green all year round.

experiment: testing an idea.

fall: the season in between summer and winter, from about September 22 to December 21 in the Northern Hemisphere and from about March 21 to June 21 in the Southern Hemisphere.

fledglings: baby birds that are learning to fly.

flyway: an air route used by migrating birds.

germination: when a seed opens and starts to grow toward light.

hydroponics: a way to grow plants in liquid without using any soil.

Glossary

hypothesis: an unproven idea that tries to explain certain facts or observations.

instinct: an inherited, natural pattern of behavior.

landmark: an object used as a point of reference so you know where you're going.

mammals: animals that make milk for their babies.

migration: the movement of groups of animals like birds or fishes from one region to another for feeding or breeding.

migratory bird: a bird that migrates.

Northern Hemisphere: the half of the earth to the north of the equator.

observe: to look at things carefully.

organism: a living thing.

photosynthesis: the way a plant makes its own food.

porous: something that has spaces inside it to absorb fluid.

predators: animals that hunt and eat other animals.

scientific process: the way scientists ask questions and do experiments to prove their ideas.

scientist: someone who studies science and knows a lot about it.

sort: to organize things into different groups.

Southern Hemisphere: the half of the earth to the south of the equator.

species: animal or plant family.

spring: the season in between winter and summer, from about March 21 to June 21 in the Northern Hemisphere and from about September 22 to December 21 in the Southern Hemisphere.

summer solstice: the longest day of the year and the first day of summer, about June 21 in the Northern Hemisphere and about December 21 in the Southern Hemisphere.

winter solstice: the shortest day of the year and the first day of winter, about December 21 in the Northern Hemisphere and about June 21 in the Southern Hemisphere.

Books

Branley, Franklyn M. *Air Is All Around You.* New York: Thomas Y. Crowell, 1962.

Branley, Franklyn M. *Down Comes The Rain.* New York: Harper Collins Publishers, 1963.

Dorros, Arthur. *Feel the Wind.* New York: Thomas Y. Crowell, 1989.

Drake, Jane and Ann Love. *Snow Amazing: Cool Facts and Warm Tales.* Canada: Tundra Books, 2004.

Elsom, Derek. *Weather Explained: A Beginner's Guide to the Elements.* New York: Henry Hold and Company, 1997.

Lerner, Carol. *A Forest Year.* New York: William Morrow and Company Inc., 1987.

McMillan, Bruce. *The Weather Sky.* New York: Farrar Straus Giroux, 1991.

McVey, Vicki. *The Sierra Club Book of Weatherwisdom.* San Francisco: Sierra Club Books and Boston, Toronto, London: Little, Brown and Co., 1991.

Pope, Joyce and Dr. Philip Whitfield. *Why Do The Seasons Change?: Questions on Nature's Rhythms and Cycles answered by the Natural History Museum.* New York: Viking Penguin Inc., 1987.

Shedd, Warner. *The Kids Wildlife Book.* Vermont: Williamson Publishing, 1994.

Simon, Seymour. *Weather.* New York: Morrow Junior Books, 1993.

Vogel, Carole G. *Nature's Fury: Eyewitness Reports of Natural Disasters.* Scholastic Inc., 2000.

Web Sites

The Weather Channel
http://www.weatherclassroom.com

Weather Wiz Kids
http://www.weatherwizkids.com

National Geographic Kids
http://kids.nationalgeographic.com

The Audubon Society
http://www.audubon.org/educate

The Museum of Science, Boston
http://www.mos.org

The Exploratorium
http://www.exploratorium.edu

USDA Forest Service
http://www.fs.fed.us

Scholastic
http://www.scholastic.com/kids/weather

Wikipedia
http://www.wikipedia.org

World Book Encyclopedia
http://www.worldbook.com/features/seasons/html/seasons.htm

The Library of Congress
http://www.loc.gov

The Academy of Natural Sciences
http://www.ansp.org

The Carnegie Science Museum
http://www.carnegiesciencecenter.org

Index

H

homes, 55–72
hydroponics, 25

I

ice, 16, 18, 20, 21, 74–76, 83
instinct, 44, 47, 56

L

lightning, 75, 78, 80, 81

M

maple syrup, 34
Methuselah Tree, 38
migration, 43–54, 70, 85
mothers, 64, 65, 69, 71
mud, 2, 83

N

nests, 1, 58–60, 62, 64
North Pole, 11, 13, 14
Northern Hemisphere, 4, 9, 11, 14, 15, 22, 74
nuts and fruit, 31–33

O

oceans, 16, 74

P

paper, 40–42
photosynthesis, 20, 22
plants, 1, 16–42, 71, 85
predators, 59, 64, 65

R

rain, 13, 16, 74–76, 82, 83
roots, 17, 18, 20–22, 26, 34

S

sap, 34
scientific process, 2
scientist, 2–5
sea creatures, 45, 46, 49
seals, 45, 46
seeds, 16, 21, 23–25
snakes, 50, 57, 71
snow, 2, 8, 74, 75, 83, 85
soil, 16–23, 25, 26, 29, 34, 74, 76, 82, 83
South Pole, 11, 13–15
Southern Hemisphere, 9, 11, 14, 15
stars, 48
storms, 75, 78–81, 83
summer, 10–12, 22, 35, 44, 45, 52, 55, 69, 70, 71
sun, 8–17, 19–24, 44, 48, 73–76, 81–83

T

thunder, thunderstorm, 78–81
tornadoes, 75, 78, 79
trees, 1, 6, 18, 30–42, 58, 62, 64, 82
tropics, 13, 32, 33, 45
turtles, 45

W

water, 16, 18, 21, 24–29, 34, 35, 74–77, 81
weather, 8, 44, 56, 73–85
whales, 45, 46, 49
wind, 74, 82, 84
winter, 3, 8, 10, 12, 13, 20, 34, 44, 52, 55, 70, 74, 85
worms, 17, 18